A Note to Parents

DK READERS is a compelling program for beginning readers, designed in conjunction with leading literacy experts, including Dr. Linda Gambrell, Director of the School of Education at Clemson University. Dr. Gambrell has served on the Board of Directors of the International Reading Association and as President of the National Reading Conference.

Beautiful illustrations and superb full-color photographs combine with engaging, easy-to-read stories to offer a fresh approach to each subject in the series. Each DK READER is guaranteed to capture a child's interest while developing his or her reading skills, general knowledge, and love of reading.

The four levels of DK READERS are aimed at different reading abilities, enabling you to choose the books that are exactly right for your child:

Level 1 – Beginning to read
Level 2 – Beginning to read alone
Level 3 – Reading alone
Level 4 – Proficient readers

The "normal" age at which a child begins to read can be anywhere from three to eight years old, so these levels are intended only as a general guideline.

No matter which level you select, you can be sure that you are helping your child learn to read, then read to learn!

A DK PUBLISHING BOOK
www.dk.com

Project Editor Mary Atkinson
Art Editor Karen Lieberman
Senior Editor Linda Esposito
Deputy Managing Art Editor Jane Horne
US Editor Regina Kahney
Production Kate Oliver
Picture Researcher Mary Sweeney
Scientific Consultant Dr. Angela Milner

Reading Consultant
Linda B. Gambrell, Ph.D.

First American Edition, 1998
06 07 08 09 20 19 18 17 16 15
Published in the United States by
DK Publishing, Inc.
375 Hudson Street, New York, New York 10014

Visit us on the World Wide Web at http://www.dk.com

Library of Congress Cataloging-in-Publication Data
Davis, Lee.
 Dinosaur dinners / written by Lee Davis.
  p. cm. -- (Eyewitness readers. Level 2)
 ISBN-13: 978-0-7894-4252-9 (PLC)
 ISBN-13: 978-0-7894-2959-9 (PB)
  1. Dinosaurs--Juvenile literature. [1. Dinosaurs.] I. Title. II. Series.
 QE862.D5T37   1998
 567.9--dc21
                                     97-36750
                                        CIP
                                        AC

Color reproduction by Colourscan, Singapore
Printed and bound in the U.S.A. by Lake Book Manufacturing

The publisher would like to thank the following:
Museums: Natural History Museum, London, and
Royal Tyrrel Museum of Palaeontology, Alberta

Artists/model makers: Roby Braun, Jim Channell, John Holmes,
Graham High/Jeremy Hunt/Centaur Studios, and Kenneth Lilly

Photographers: Andy Crawford, John Downs,
Neil Fletcher, Dave King, Tim Ridley, and Dave Rudkin.

READERS

BEGINNING TO READ ALONE
2

Dinosaur Dinners

Written by Lee Davis

DK Publishing, Inc.

I am a dinosaur
looking for my breakfast.

I can see you,
wherever you are.

A deadly dinosaur
Troodon was a quick
and clever hunter.
It had large eyes for spotting
prey, even in dim light.

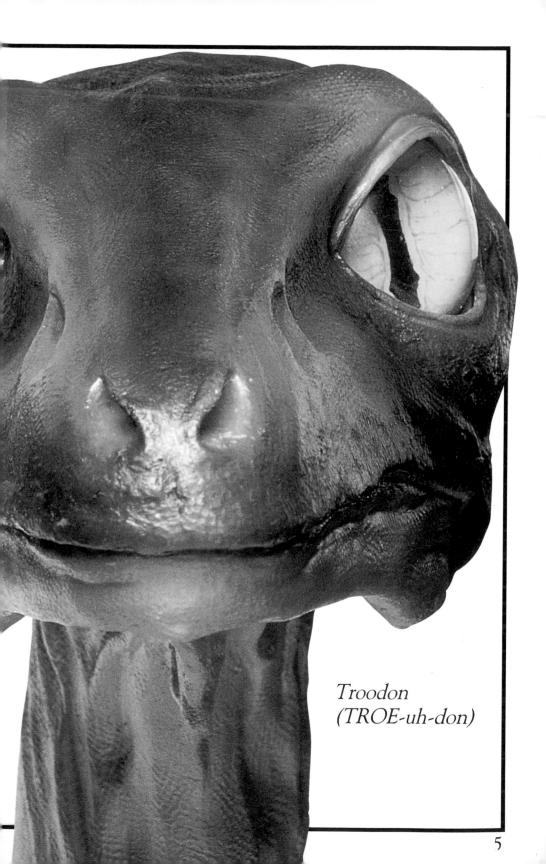

Troodon
(TROE-uh-don)

I am a dinosaur
ready for my lunch.

*Herrerasaurus
(her-RARE-uh-SORE-us)*

I can catch you,
even if you run.

A speedy sprinter

Herrerasaurus ran fast
on its two back legs.
It hunted small reptiles,
such as lizards.

I am a dinosaur,
hungry for my dinner.
And I am bigger than you are.

A huge hunter

Tyrannosaurus was one of
the biggest meat-eating
dinosaurs ever. It was as tall
as a two-story building.

Tyrannosaurus
(tie-RAN-uh-SORE-us)

We all have
sharp teeth and claws.
We are meat eaters.
We eat other dinosaurs.

Tyrannosaurus

Troodon

Herrerasaurus

Hungry for meat

Meat-eating dinosaurs ate fish, insects, small mammals, reptiles, and other dinosaurs. They are called carnivores.

Eat or be eaten?
That is the dinosaur question.

I can run fast enough to get away
from the big meat eaters.
I can also run fast enough
to catch small animals.

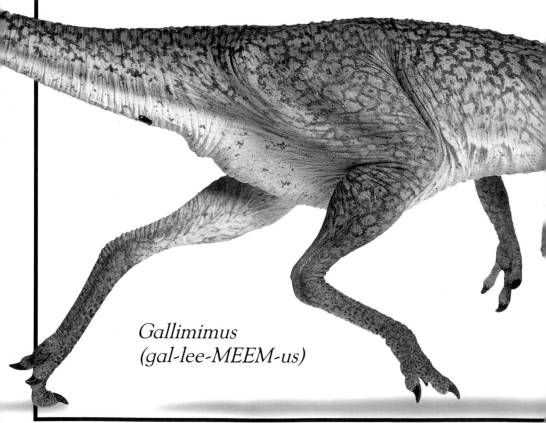

Gallimimus
(gal-lee-MEEM-us)

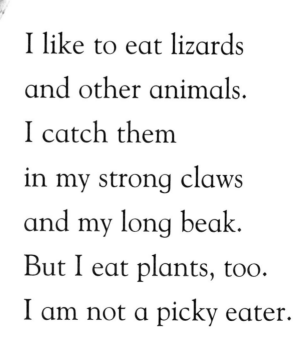

A mixed diet

Gallimimus snapped up leaves and small animals in its beak. It is called an omnivore because it ate both plants and meat.

I like to eat lizards
and other animals.
I catch them
in my strong claws
and my long beak.
But I eat plants, too.
I am not a picky eater.

I am a dinosaur
who eats nothing but plants.
I stay close to my babies
to protect them from meat eaters.

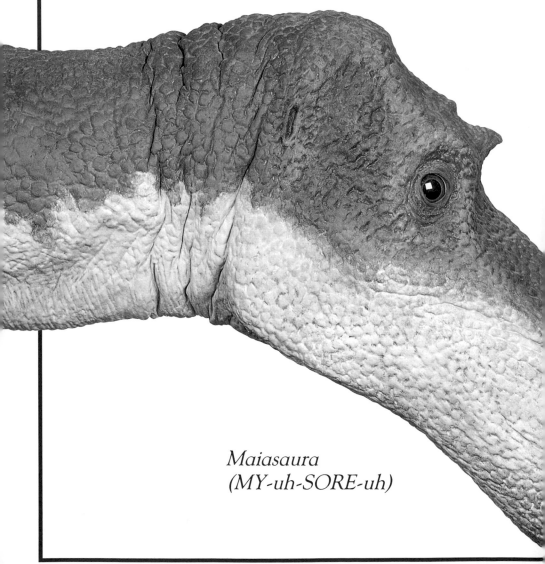

Maiasaura
(MY-uh-SORE-uh)

Eggs in a nest

Dinosaurs laid eggs
in nests on the ground.
Their babies hatched out
of the eggs, just like
baby birds and crocodiles.

I made their nest

from a mound of earth.

I bring leaves and berries

for them to eat.

Dinosaurs that don't eat meat
need protection from those that do.
Our spikes are long and sharp.
If meat eaters come too close,
we take them on head first.

Dinos and rhinos

Styracosaurus had
a long horn on its nose.
It used the horn
for protection,
like the rhinoceros does today.

Styracosaurus
(sty-RAK-uh-SORE-us)

Sharp teeth cannot dent
my body armor.
And watch out for the spikes
on my shoulders.
One bump from me and
it's the end.

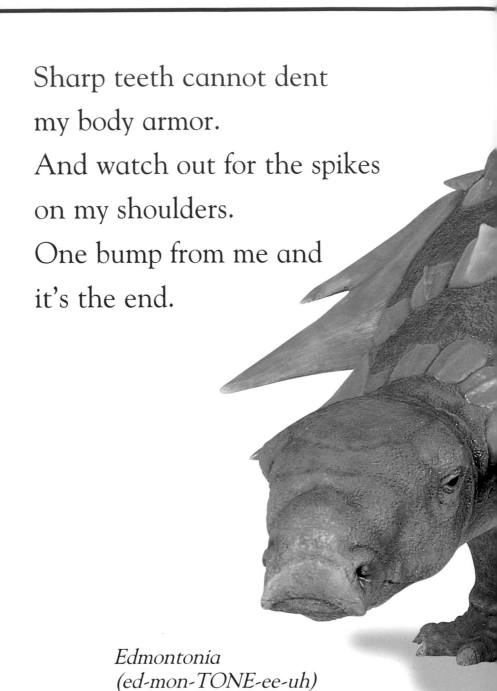

Edmontonia
(ed-mon-TONE-ee-uh)

My skin is as hard as a rock.
My body is covered
in studs, spikes, and horns.

I swing the club
on the end of my tail.
It can break the legs
of the bigger dinosaurs.

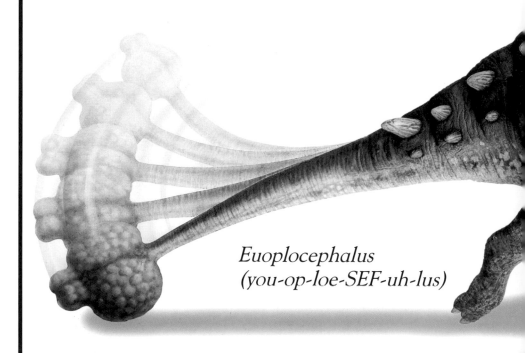

Euoplocephalus
(you-op-loe-SEF-uh-lus)

Bone-breaking bones

A tail club could grow
as wide as an armchair.
It was a powerful weapon
against meat eaters.

I am not very big,

but I am dangerous.

We are small but fast.
We eat plants that
grow close to the ground.

We live in a herd.

If one of us spots a meat eater,

we all zoom off

on our strong back legs.

Hypsilophodon
(hip-si-LOAF-uh-don)

We don't need special weapons.
If we smell danger,
we raise the alarm.
We use our head crests like trumpets
to make loud hooting calls.

Fancy heads

Other dinosaurs had
crests on their heads, too.
Often the males had bigger
crests than the females.

Parasaurolophus
(par-uh-sore-oh-LOAF-us)

Corythosaurus
(koe-rith-uh-SORE-us)

I look frightening
because I am so big.

I need to eat
huge amounts of leaves
to keep myself going.
I use my long neck
to reach the leaves
at the tops of trees.

Barosaurus
(bar-uh-SORE-us)

I can see danger coming
from any direction.
I am much taller
than any of the meat eaters.

We are all dinosaurs that eat plants. We all have some way of protecting ourselves from meat eaters.

Barosaurus

Styracosaurus

Euoplocephalus

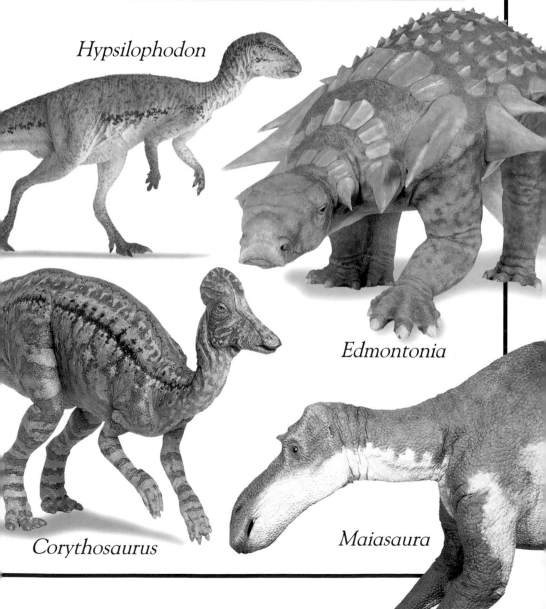

Plant lovers

Animals that eat nothing but
plants are called herbivores.
Most of the dinosaurs
were herbivores.

Hypsilophodon

Edmontonia

Corythosaurus

Maiasaura

We are all dinosaurs.
What do we eat for dinner?

Dinosaur Glossary

Barosaurus (bar-uh-SORE-us)
- name means "heavy lizard"
- a herbivore (plant eater)
- 89 feet (27 meters) long
- lived 150 million years ago

Corythosaurus (koe-rith-uh-SORE-us)
- name means "helmet lizard"
- a herbivore
- 33 feet (10 meters) long
- lived 75 million years ago

Edmontonia (ed-mon-TONE-ee-uh)
- name means "from Edmonton" (Canada)
- a herbivore
- 23 feet (7 meters) long
- lived 74–72 million years ago

Euoplocephalus (you-op-loe-SEF-uh-lus)
- name means "well-armored head"
- a herbivore
- 23 feet (7 meters) long
- lived 73 million years ago

Gallimimus (gal-lee-MEEM-us)
- name means "chicken mimic"
- an omnivore (plant and meat eater)
- 20 feet (6 meters) long
- lived 73 million years ago

Herrerasaurus (her-RARE-uh-SORE-us)
- name means "Herrera's lizard" after Victorino Herrera who discovered it
- a carnivore (meat eater)
- 10 feet (3 meters) long
- lived 228 million years ago

Hypsilophodon (hip-si-LOAF-uh-don)
- name means "high ridge tooth"
- a herbivore
- 7–8 feet (2–2.5 meters) long
- lived 120 million years ago

Maiasaura (MY-uh-SORE-uh)
- name means "good mother lizard"
- a herbivore
- 30 feet (9 meters) long
- lived 80–75 million years ago

Parasaurolophus (par-uh-sore-oh-LOAF-us)
- name means "beside ridge lizard"
- a herbivore
- 33 feet (10 meters) long
- lived 75–70 million years ago

Styracosaurus (sty-RAK-uh-SORE-us)
- name means "spiked lizard"
- a herbivore
- 18 feet (5.5 meters) long
- lived 75–72 million years ago

Troodon (TROE-uh-don)
- name means "wounding tooth"
- a carnivore
- 6 feet (2 meters) long
- lived 73–65 million years ago

Tyrannosaurus (tie-RAN-uh-SORE-us)
- name means "tyrant lizard"
- a carnivore
- 39 feet (12 meters) long
- lived 67–65 million years ago